CHILDREN
GROWING UP WITH
WAR

JENNY MATTHEWS

CANDLEWICK PRESS

CONTENTS

Text and photographs copyright © 2014 by Jenny Matthews
Design copyright © 2014 by Franklin Watts

First U.S. edition 2014

Library of Congress Catalog Card Number pending
ISBN 978-0-7636-6942-3

SCP 19 18 17 16 15 14
10 9 8 7 6 5 4 3 2 1

Printed in Humen, Dongguan, China

This book was typeset in Adobe Garamond.

Candlewick Press
99 Dover Street
Somerville, Massachusetts 02144

visit us at www.candlewick.com

"FOR ALL THOSE CHILDREN WHOSE LIVES HAVE BEEN TOUCHED BY WAR, MAY THEIR FUTURES BE MARKED BY PEACE.
MAY THOSE WHO HAVE HAD HAPPY PEACEFUL CHILDHOODS, BE INSPIRED TO THINK ABOUT CHANGING THE WORLD.
TO THOSE OF YOU WHO WANT TO BE PHOTOGRAPHERS, POWER TO YOUR PICTURES." J.M.

Countries highlighted in **bold** have an explanation of how conflict has affected them on pages 46–47.

INTRODUCTION

WHY AM I A PHOTOGRAPHER?

I became a photographer more than thirty years ago because I wanted to change the world. Since then I have traveled to many conflict zones to take photographs. Unfortunately, taking pictures rarely changes anything, but it has given me a way to communicate. I can tell people's stories and hope that my photos will encourage others to get involved—either by giving money, voting, lobbying politicians, or becoming a voice against injustice.

The main focus of my work is to document what goes on behind the frontline, and how it affects women, children, and families in their day-to-day lives.

CHILDREN AND WAR

How would you feel if you lost your home and had to flee from your own country? Imagine losing some or all of your family, either as a direct result of fighting or indirectly through illness and disease. You might have to work to support your family or fight and kill other people just to survive. And how can you go to school if it's being used as an army command outpost and all the books have been destroyed?

This is the reality for too many children and their families in the world. Today, children are still growing up with war—the consequences of which they'll live with for the rest of their lives.

This book features just some of the thousands of photographs I've taken. They've been split up to show different ways in which children are affected by war. These children don't make war, but are dragged into it—usually by adults, and usually by men. These children are supposed to be protected by the UN Convention on the Rights of the Child—see page 5—but each of the ways we see children affected is a violation of their rights.

▲ *These are press cards that I needed to work as a journalist in Sudan and Israel.*

WORKING FREELANCE

I'm a freelance photojournalist, which means I don't work for a particular company or organization. Sometimes, I accompany a journalist on a story for a magazine or newspaper. At other times, I'm commissioned by non-governmental organizations (NGOs), such as ActionAid or CARE International, that provide emergency help. They need photographs to inform the public and raise money. Other times I travel to places to work on a major project of my own, looking at women and war.

◄ *Many countries I travel to require visas. These pages from my passport show the visas I had for **Uganda** and Chad.*

▶ *This hamsa, or hand of Fatima (hand of Miriam in Judaism), was a present I received in **Iraq**. I like to think it protects me on my assignments.*

GETTING INTO A CONFLICT ZONE

Often, the biggest challenge for a journalist is the logistics of getting to a trouble spot and working safely once there. Research is essential. I use the library and Internet for background information and watch news reports, talk to experts, and learn a bit of the language.

Local people are invaluable. Sometimes I pay a "fixer"—a local person with good contacts—to help me find people and places and to translate. At other times, I work with local organizations. I try to travel as discreetly as possible, but in some dangerous situations photographers team up for safety and support and to share travel expenses.

▲ *Unlike me, Farida, who I worked with in* **Afghanistan**, *knew that the red-and-white stones meant the road had just been demined, and was safe to walk along.*

This is my essential camera equipment. I try to travel as lightly as possible, taking only carry-on luggage if it's a short trip. The less you carry, the faster you can move (especially getting on and off planes!).

Card reader

Memory cards

Portable hard drive for storing and backing up downloaded pictures

USB hard drive that can be taken to a shop to get prints made

60 mm macro lens

Flash

18–200 mm lens

Laptop computer for downloading photos on memory cards

12–24 mm wide-angle lens

Lens cleaner

Spare batteries

Digital SLR camera

▲ *On every trip, I carry a notebook for keeping a record of places, people, and their comments. If I have time, I write a diary.*

▶ *Money from some of the places I have visited. It's important to have local currency—you can't pay by debit card in most places.*

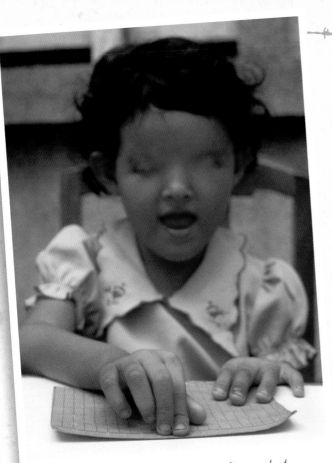

It was very emotional to realize what Phuong had been denied—the very sense that I rely on for my work.

FINDING PHUONG

The effects of war hit home to me when I was photographing in Vietnam long after the war was over. In the 1960s, the situation in this country shaped my political views and made me aware of the part that film and photography play in recording history.

When I visited an orphanage in Saigon, one little girl named Phuong was wearing sunglasses. When she took them off, I was shocked to see that she had no eyes.

It is presumed that her mother was poisoned by Agent Orange, a chemical sprayed by U.S. planes over forests during the Vietnam War. The chemical remains in the ecosystem and continues to cause birth defects.

" Although I may shoot a photograph in 125th of a second—so all the photos in this book add up to less than a minute—I spent hours traveling, chatting, and listening before I took them. "

The UN Convention on the Rights of the Child is an agreement which gives everyone under the age of eighteen key rights designed to help protect them. Unfortunately, war can mean that these rights are forgotten, leaving children vulnerable to abuse and violence.

- The right to enjoy these rights, regardless of race, color, sex, religion, national or social origin
- The right to develop individual abilities
- The right to a name and nationality
- The right to adequate nutrition and medical care
- The right to special care if disabled
- The right to affection, love, and understanding
- The right to free education, to learn to be a useful member of society, and to full opportunity for play and recreation
- The right to be among the first to receive relief in times of disaster
- The right to protection against all forms of neglect, cruelty, and exploitation
- The right to be brought up in a spirit of peace

How many of these rights do you think would be affected by war?

▲ *These boys have made their own toy guns from wood and other scrap materials.*

HOME AND DISPLACEMENT

When there's a war going on, some people have no choice but to stay in their house or apartment and hope they will not be bombed or attacked. If possible, families flee. They might end up constructing temporary homes, sleeping in a school, camping in a park, or renting rooms in another town within their country. These people become known as internally displaced persons (IDPs).

If people cross an international border, they become refugees. If they are lucky, the international community provides help—although appeals rarely raise enough funds. Refugees sell jewelry and other valuables to survive.

THE NUMBER OF PEOPLE DISPLACED BY WAR IN 2012

15.4 million refugees

28.8 million IDPs

Source: UN Global Trends 2013

In the **Democratic Republic of the Congo (DRC)**, *displaced people constructed temporary homes out of branches and plastic sheeting.*

KIBATI CAMP FOR THE DISPLACED, GOMA, DRC, NOVEMBER 2008

I went to Goma in the DRC to report on the humanitarian crisis facing the people there. Terrorized communities had fled from rebels and ended up in camps. Here, they had to build improvised shelters for themselves on hard, uncomfortable volcanic rock. As I walked around, I spotted Fraha, resplendent in an orange dress and scarf, sitting next to her hut with her baby son, Shukuru. I am always impressed by how women in the most difficult conditions take pride in their appearance. They are neat and clean despite having no electricity or running water. A nearby family asked me to photograph them in front of their new home.

▲ *Fraha and her baby, Shukuru.*

▲ *Nyirrahabimana (second from left) is proud of the shelter she built with her sister Maombi (right) for themselves and their children from bits of scrap wood and old plastic food sacks.*

7

DEKWANEH, BEIRUT, LEBANON, AUGUST 2006

When pieces of paper came fluttering down onto her apartment block, Lina knew instantly what they meant. On each one was a message from the Israeli army telling people to leave the area of Dahiyeh, a poor district of Beirut, before a bombing raid began. Lina grabbed her two daughters, three-year-old Aya and four-month-old Maia, and stuffed some clothes into a plastic bag. She left a message for her husband, who was at work, and fled to a school in nearby Dekwaneh. Throughout Beirut and the southern towns of Tyre and Sidon, hundreds of schools offered shelter to people like Lina, who had suddenly become homeless.

Lina, Aya, and Maia camp in a classroom, thankful to have a roof over their heads, but uncertain of when they'll be able to return home.

▲ *The hoses used for watering the plants in the park came in handy for washing clothes and keeping cool in the boiling summer heat.*

SANAYEH GARDEN, BEIRUT, LEBANON, AUGUST 2006

Hundreds of other families, including Azzat and her eight children, were forced to camp on the grass in a local park. In the middle of the night the bomber planes flew over. The explosions as bombs landed and destroyed buildings were terrifying.

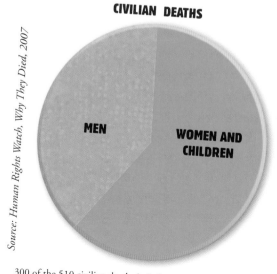

CIVILIAN DEATHS

Source: Human Rights Watch, Why They Died, 2007

MEN

WOMEN AND CHILDREN

300 of the 510 civilian deaths in **Lebanon** during the 34-day conflict with Israel were women and children.

▲ *I was standing next to Azzat on a Sunday afternoon when a bomb dropped nearby. She grabbed a child and froze in complete panic.*

RAMADA REFUGEE CAMP, TUNISIA, MAY 2011

In the rush to flee **Libya** for the safety of a refugee camp just over the border in Tunisia, Mona forgot her acne cream. It's the one thing she wishes she'd grabbed. Now she's living in a tent, sleeping on a mat on the sand without even a change of clothes. And her skin isn't getting better, but she also has more serious things to think about.

"We've left behind our family, our homes, our goods. It's not a life here. In Nalut we had a lovely home. Here we can only read the Qur'an, tidy up, and organize play activities for the younger children. Because we fled in fear, we left everything behind, so we only have the clothes we are wearing. We've been praying for our families in Nalut. We've been very worried. This morning, before sunrise, we felt the vibrations from the mortars. I prayed for my home, my street. I prayed for hope, for my goals. My brother is fighting with a group of friends. They all look out for each other. It's been over a month since I saw him, but my father goes back when the fighting dies down and says he's in good health and really keen to carry on fighting."

▲ *Nineteen-year-old Mona outside her tent. She wanted to hide her identity to protect her family, who are still in Libya.*

▲ *More than 1,500 people spent several months living in these overcrowded tents in Ramada.*

AMMAN, JORDAN, APRIL 2013

Although many refugees seek safety in camps in a neighboring country, many others make their way to towns and cities. Here, they find shelter with family members or rent rooms and try to find work. If a conflict goes on for a long time, as in the case of **Syria**, this can put a strain on families and their finances.

When I asked some Syrian refugees in Jordan what they had brought with them when they fled from their homes, everyone said just a small bag of clothes. One family had a single room to sleep eighteen people. Each night they unfurled neatly folded blankets to make the floor a bit more comfortable.

▲ *This family could only afford to rent a single room. There is no fridge, no washing machine, no stove—there isn't even a bathroom.*

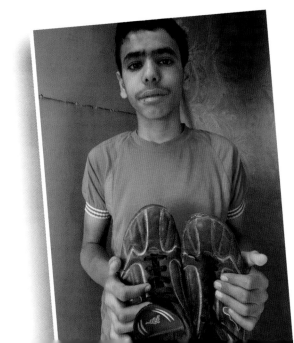

◀ *Hassan, age fifteen, explained to me that he brought only the clothes he was wearing and a pair of shoes.*

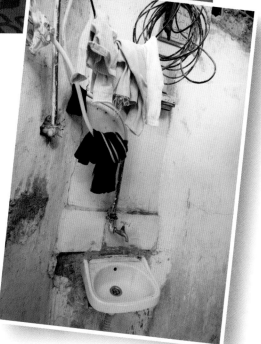

▲ *Everyone shares a single toilet and a sink for washing.*

11

THE PHOTOGRAPHER'S PERSPECTIVE

I'm aware that, as a photographer, I "parachute" into people's lives and spend a short amount of time talking, listening, and photographing. Then I leave them and go back to a world with electricity, running water, a choice of what to eat, and the freedom to travel. I think it's easy to forget how lucky we are. When I'm taking photographs I have to focus on the reason I'm there: to report back, to get my photos published, and to share information and stories with the rest of the world.

In 2007, I traveled to Goz Bagar camp in Chad for CARE. I was there to photograph the work they were doing with Sudanese refugees who had fled from the conflict in **Darfur**. They use my photographs to illustrate stories and articles on their website and in their promotional materials.

While I was at Goz Bagar camp, I met a mother and her family. She had left everything behind in Sudan, and I recorded what she said to me in one of my notebooks:

Mariam Issak Adam, age thirty, with her four children—Ousman Issak, age ten; Nadjoi Issak, age seven; Mahama Issak, age five; and Yakhoub Issak, age three—at Goz Bagar camp.

"The war sent us from our village. Before we had breakfast, armed men came to our village. They killed nine people, including my husband, and so we decided to leave because of the lack of security. Life is difficult now. I've lost my husband and I've my children to look after. I've no hope of going back. The men who attacked us are still there, next to the village. I brought nothing with us, no money, no goods, nothing."

Refugee women often stand for hours in the hot sun waiting to receive their monthly ration of flour, sugar, and oil. Being a refugee means eating what you are given and hoping there will be enough to last until the next distribution.

LIFE FOR REFUGEES

The difference between my life and that of refugees is enormous. I am always very humbled that people who have lost virtually everything can be bothered to talk to me about their lives, and insist on sharing what little they have—always offering me food and tea.

In Qawala camp, near Sulaimaniya, Kurdistan, in 2008, I met three-year-old Taybeh and her mother. They fled from the sectarian violence between Sunnis and Shiites in northern Iraq. The camp was home to around three thousand people, just some of the 2.5 million Iraqis who are homeless in their own country.

▲ *Taybeh and her mother live on a landfill site in a structure made from an old tent and plastic sheeting. I think they were laughing at me for taking a photo of them washing dishes. At home they'd had a full kitchen, with running water, and a washing machine.*

Tahane stands with her children in front of her home. She's come back to see what she can salvage from the ruins.

PERMANENT CAMPS

Sometimes people spend a few months in tents. Others, like the Palestinians in Gaza and the West Bank, build houses where their tents were but still refer to their communities as "camps," even though they've lived there for more than sixty years.

I met Tahane in Netzarim, Gaza, in 2009 after the Israeli Defense Forces launched Operation Cast Lead. She told me how announcements over loudspeakers had told her to leave her house. She had just enough time to pack a few things and scoop up her three young children before the air strike. Her house was completely destroyed.

WHO ARE REFUGEES?

Source: UNHCR Global Trends Report 2012

Forty-six percent of refugees in 2012 were children under the age of eighteen.

FAMILY

War breaks families apart through anxiety, separation, and death. Traditionally, many fathers are killed. This can be devastating for children, and life for the family becomes much harder, especially if he was the only one earning money.

Increasingly, though, different types of conflict mean that children are being caught up in war in other ways, such as when missiles miss their targets and hit children, as happened to Nabeela's family. In some cases, young people are sent away for safety and grow up without their parents. Others are kidnapped and forced to become soldiers. Entire families can become casualties of war.

▲ *Nabeela (from Gaza) holds a photo of her twelve-year-old son Mohammed, who was killed by a bomb that injured her other two sons. One lost an eye and the other lost both legs.*

▲ *Ali (from Iraq) with a photograph of his son, who disappeared on his way to Australia. Ali thinks he might have been among a group of asylum seekers whose boat sank.*

MEDENINE TRANSIT CENTER FOR LIBYAN REFUGEES, TUNISIA, MAY 2011

Afaf is the mother of six young children. Her husband was killed in Libya fighting Colonel Muammar Gaddafi's regime. Having fled to Tunisia for safety, she now faces change in her country as head of the family.

▲ *Afaf holds a photograph of her husband, who was killed in Libya.*

"We come from the city of Nalut, up on the mountain. We ran away because of the bombing. We are not running away because we are afraid of death, but because we women fear being attacked. The men brought the women here and went back to fight. My husband, Abdul Hameed, was killed in Nalut. He taught mechanics and had experience of guns because he did his national service. He was an instructor to other rebels. We want Libya to change. First, we want decent education. The children's life is zero. We want a good economy and a good health system. I want a good future for my children."

AFGHANISTAN, 2009

In many places, decades of war have created a culture of violence. People are killed over petty arguments and children are used to solve family problems.

In Afghanistan there is a tradition called "baad," whereby a girl is given away to solve a dispute. In 2009, I met Hulya, a fourteen-year-old girl, whose father had killed his brother in a fight over some wood. To stop the two families from fighting, Hulya was married to her fifteen-year-old cousin Humdillah.

Young girls are also used to rescue families from the poverty that can result from conflict. When a marriage is arranged, the bride's family receives a bride price, and this money can make a big difference to them. For widows, though, it is hard to negotiate a good bride price and ensure their daughters are treated well. Women can be mistreated by their husbands, and some run away.

▲ *Neither Humdillah nor Hulya wants to be married, but they have no choice.*

Angiza (not her real name) ran away from an uncle who was trying to sell her in Kabul. Fortunately, she was able to find a safe shelter, which is very unusual in a country with no social services. Women are often put in prison for running away.

▲ *Sahat Gul has arranged for her daughter, ten-year-old Gul, to marry a middle-aged man.*

▲ *Sefura with two of her daughters and one of her sons. Her youngest daughter holds a photo of her father.*

When I met Sefura in Kabul, Afghanistan, she was saddened both by the loss of her husband and by the effect it had on her daughters' lives.

"The Taliban killed my husband in 2001. He was in the military. I have four daughters and two sons. The sons work pushing carts and selling vegetables. Five months after I was widowed, my sixteen-year-old daughter disappeared. She had been engaged since she was three months old. I don't know what happened to her. Her fiancé's family was furious. They demanded two daughters in her place and forced two of my daughters to marry. There was nothing I could do. If my husband had not died, we could have looked after our first daughter better, so she would not have disappeared. He could have protected us. It is because I am a widow that all these things have happened."

War, and the subsequent loss of family members, makes children grow up too quickly. They lose their childhood and take on adult roles, including that of soldier. In many recent wars in Africa, particularly those in **Sierra Leone**, Liberia, Uganda, and the DRC, children have been drugged and forced to kill. These children sometimes spend years in "small boy units" and adapt to their environment and the power they get from using weapons. It is very difficult to reintegrate them back into their communities afterward.

▲ *Clutching a Kalashnikov gun, this young boy is guarding a restaurant in Freetown, the capital of Sierra Leone.*

CASE STUDY: PEACE CLUB, BARLONYO, UGANDA, 2011

Susan, a young mother, is part of a peace club in Barlonyo. It's a group of former child abductees who support one another and reenact the massacre carried out by the Lord's Resistance Army (LRA) to explain to the community what happened and why there has to be reconciliation.

Susan is dressed up as Joseph Kony (below), the leader of the LRA. Kony is responsible for abducting thousands of children in northern Uganda and turning them into child soldiers who then terrorized and killed villagers.

Susan is familiar with the LRA. They abducted her and forced her to kill a baby. Although only a child herself, she had to become the "wife" of an LRA soldier. When the Ugandan army rescued her, she was pregnant. She now has a seven-year-old son.

Susan acts the part of Kony.

Barlonyo, Susan's community, was the scene of a massacre in 2004. The LRA commander launched an operation called "Kill Every Living Thing" at a camp for displaced villagers. There were lots of young people in the camp, and the LRA wanted to abduct them and force them to become part of their group.

That afternoon, more than three hundred people were burned inside their straw huts and hacked to death with machetes. Hundreds of young people were taken away.

After years living in the bush with the LRA, it was very hard for children who had been kidnapped by the LRA to return to their communities once the war ended. They felt guilty, and many villagers blamed them for killing their family members.

Boys act the part of abducted child soldiers.

▲ *Young people playing the part of villagers are roped together and taken away to be "shot."*

THE PHOTOGRAPHER'S PERSPECTIVE

▲ *Samah, her husband, Darwish, and their four children fled from Syria to Jordan in April 2013.*

People often ask me how I can bear to work in difficult situations. I think it helps that I know *why* I am taking pictures. Some people think a journalist should be a neutral, uninvolved observer, just writing or photographing. For me, I want to be as close as possible to my subjects in order to try to understand what people are going through. This usually means taking sides. It also means spending time with people — which they really value — and taking time to listen and observe.

As a photographer I want to portray intimate situations, but at the same time the camera distances me — there is a lens between me and reality. Sometimes this means it is possible to photograph something quite horrible and save my emotional reaction to it for later.

▶ *Fatem and her teddy. Fatem's mother said, "The area was being attacked, so we hid in a shelter. As I left the house, my two-year-old daughter grabbed her teddy. She held on as tightly to the teddy as she did to me, so we couldn't leave it behind. Her father gave it to her on her first birthday."*

I think this way of making sense of each situation enabled me to work in **Rwanda** when I traveled there during the genocide in 1994.

GENOCIDE IN RWANDA, 1994

More than 800,000 people were killed in Rwanda during the hundred days of genocide in 1994. Every family has a story of loss and pain—some lost twenty relatives, some thirty. They were all killed in the most savage ways. At the time, Rwanda seemed to be a country of widows and orphans.

The people who did the killing, and others who were part of their community and saw what happened, fled over the border to neighboring Zaire (now the DRC). Lots of children were separated from their families on the long walk to the border. It is thought some families deliberately "lost" their small children, either knowing they could move faster without them or hoping they would be taken care of by a foreign aid agency and therefore have a better future.

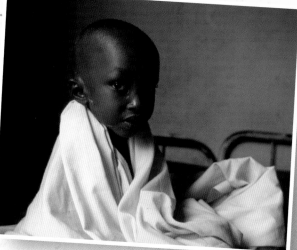

▲ *I came across five-year-old Kamonzi in a hospital. He is one of the thousands of orphans traumatized by what they have seen and unable to speak.*

"Sometimes I do stop taking photos and help. No picture is worth someone dying for. Life is always more important than photography."

▲ *When you see an abandoned child, your instinct is to help—to take them somewhere safe. In an emergency situation there might not be many options. During a cholera epidemic in Zaire, the only possibility for this child was one of the tents that some aid workers set up as an orphanage.*

▲ *In Sierra Leone, rebels (young boys, often high on drugs) terrorized and mutilated people with knives—often cutting off their hands. Mariatu, age fifteen (left), and Adamasay, age fourteen (right), survived, but many others bled to death because there were no doctors or nurses with equipment to save them. Mariatu is now a UNICEF Special Representative for Children and Armed Conflict.*

HEALTH

In the course of war, bodies and minds are damaged and destroyed. Besides deaths from bombings and guns, many people die because of poor health facilities; hospitals, clinics, and even ambulances are often destroyed. It might even be too dangerous to take people to get treatment.

People's health is also affected by the poverty that war brings. Adults lose their jobs and therefore their income. As a result, people, especially children, die from hunger or from lack of access to medical facilities and even clean water. In the

▲ Parents whose babies died of hunger pray with members of the community at their graves in the Syakamak village cemetery in Afghanistan.

camps set up in Zaire after the Rwanda genocide, there was a massive cholera epidemic caused by the lack of toilets and clean water.

Because of stress and anxiety, women often give birth prematurely in conflict situations and then have to care for newborn babies in dirty conditions. I've seen babies die because their mothers had no milk to feed to them. Young children have no choice but to drink dirty water. They get sick and quickly become dehydrated. Normally, this could be easily treated with a solution of salt and sugar — but this works only if the water is clean. Health programs become disrupted in wartime, too. Without vaccines, children become vulnerable to diseases such as measles, that they would normally be immunized against.

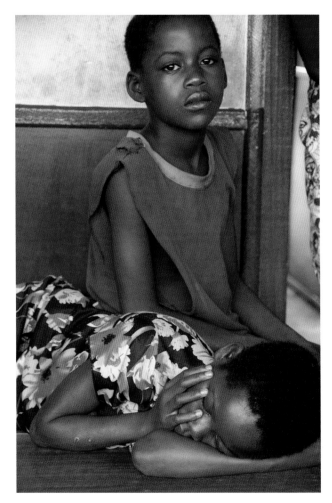

◀ A young refugee from the DRC with malaria waits to see a nurse in a village clinic. Sleeping under an insecticide-treated net greatly reduces the chances of getting malaria, which is fatal if not treated. During conflict, people do not prioritize the use of nets.

▼ Invented by French researchers, Plumpy'Nut is a soft peanut-based paste. It is high in calories and rich in protein, so children with acute malnutrition can gain weight very quickly.

War brings other health hazards, too. Dangerous chemicals, such as depleted uranium used in shells fired in Iraq, can remain in the ecosystem and affect people's health years later. Children collect scrap metal to sell and play in burned-out military vehicles, which can be highly radioactive. This poisons their bodies and can lead to cancer or birth defects when they have their own children.

▲ *A girl in Basra, Iraq, walks past a troop carrier, which still measured considerable radiation a year after being hit by a depleted-uranium-tipped rocket.*

Some weapons, such as small land mines, are designed to kill and injure soldiers. But these are left in the ground long after any war has ended. When children in Afghanistan picked up what they thought were plastic butterflies, they ended up being badly injured. Even after years of painstaking work clearing and defusing land mines, many still remain hidden.

◄ *In some countries, more than 30 percent of land mine casualties are under the age of fifteen. Shabnam, an Afghan, is one of them.*

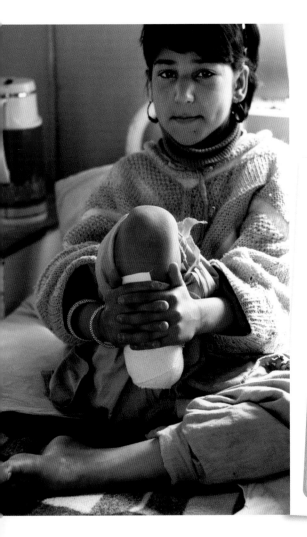

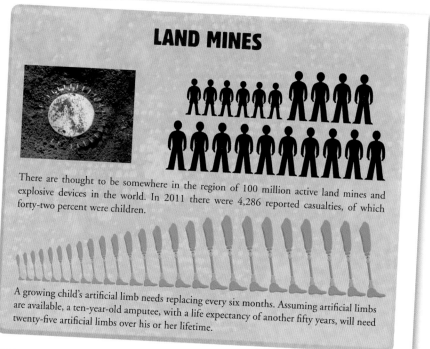

LAND MINES

There are thought to be somewhere in the region of 100 million active land mines and explosive devices in the world. In 2011 there were 4,286 reported casualties, of which forty-two percent were children.

A growing child's artificial limb needs replacing every six months. Assuming artificial limbs are available, a ten-year-old amputee, with a life expectancy of another fifty years, will need twenty-five artificial limbs over his or her lifetime.

Sources: International Campaign to Ban Landmines and One World/CARE

CASE STUDY: MENTAL HEALTH, BAOBAB CENTRE, LONDON 2013

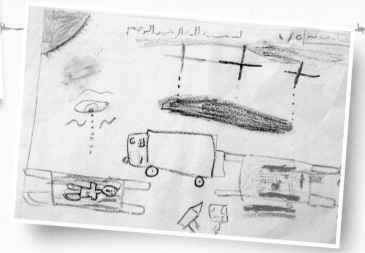

Besides physical disabilities, the stress and fear of living with war can cause children to have nightmares, to lose their confidence, and experience long-term damage to their sense of security and comfort.

The Baobab Centre for Young Survivors in Exile works with young asylum-seekers who have arrived unaccompanied in the U.K. Many of them have witnessed conflict, and some have been forced to perpetrate violence. The center provides therapy and practical support to help them deal with the lasting trauma.

When I asked students at the center in London to hold something that expressed their hope for the future, these were some of their choices:

▲ *Night after night of heavy bombing terrified everyone. This drawing shows one child's view of the violence that occurred during nights of heavy bombing in Lebanon.*

SCISSORS
"I want to be a high-fashion hairdresser. That's my future."

A JUG OF WATER
"The water is clean and clear—so I hope my future will be fine and good, not like the problems I had back home. This water represents a good future when everything will be fine."

EMPTY HANDS
"The future is blurry. Anything could happen. There's no certainty to it."

BOOK AND PEN
"My dream is to continue my education."

GUITAR AND BALLS
"Music is inspiration. Soccer and basketball are the whole world."

MONEY
"Money is life. No money, no life. Money is food. If you don't have money, you can't buy your travel card, you can't buy clothes, you can't eat."

FOLDER OF COLLEGE WORK
"Education is the key. I love geography, because it gives an understanding of how the world today is evolving."

THE PHOTOGRAPHER'S PERSPECTIVE

I think many people take health care for granted. If we need a doctor, dentist, or optometrist, we just make an appointment. In a conflict zone, getting medical help is not so easy. As a journalist, it is important that I stay healthy so that I don't become a burden on others. I carry a basic first-aid kit containing things such as aspirin and bandages.

▲ *Girls clean latrines in the DRC. Several of the doors are missing, giving users no privacy. Thirty percent of refugee camps do not have adequate latrines. Sharing a latrine with three or more families greatly increases the risk of cholera.*

Refugees in camps can often get access to these things too, but other essentials can be harder to find. Mosquitoes spread the disease malaria, so it is important to sleep under a mosquito net. Often there aren't enough nets for everybody who needs one, especially children and pregnant women. Cholera is another terrible disease, often spread by poor hygiene and dirty drinking water. I'm very careful to drink clean water, but the toilets can be a problem — it's best not to be squeamish, and a long skirt can be very useful!

At the Za'atri camp in Jordan for Syrian refugees, Qamar collects water for her family. The United Nations Refugee Agency (UNHCR) estimates that more than half of all refugee camps cannot provide the recommended daily minimum of five gallons (twenty liters) of water per person per day.

CASE STUDY: TRAINING MIDWIVES, AFGHANISTAN, 2011

One of the most memorable trips I've taken was with Merlin, a medical nongovernmental organization (NGO), to visit a training school for midwives in Afghanistan. Teenage girls spend eighteen months training and then return to work in their villages, where they are often the only health-care workers. Much of Afghanistan is very difficult to access because of high mountains and bad winter weather. Road blocks, fear of kidnapping, and lack of transportation mean women are unlikely to go to a hospital to give birth, so these midwives are essential.

I spent a week with the young women during their training, but it was considered too dangerous for me to go with a midwife to a village to see her in action. A Western photographer could have jeopardized the midwife's work and provoked the local Taliban into attacking. For me, it was more important for them to continue working safely—although it was disappointing not to follow my story to its end.

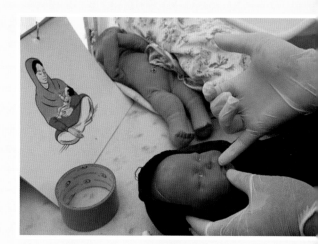

▲ *Learning to check a newborn's breathing.*

▲ *Girls learn to administer injections by practicing on tangerines.*

This newly trained midwife is about to set off to her village.

WORK

Parents always hope that their children will have a better life than their own. They want them to have a good education and a safe upbringing. But many families only survive because of the help their children provide by doing unpaid jobs such as farm work, collecting water and firewood, and looking after siblings or the family's animals.

War makes the situation worse when the family income is reduced. This can happen if a parent is away fighting or loses their job as a result of the upheavals brought by conflict. Electricity may be cut off, so workplaces close. Children can end up begging or helping someone out in return for food.

▲ *In refugee camps, like this one in the Central African Republic (CAR), girls don't have to walk as far to get water as they would in their villages. However, they are still likely to miss school as they wait in the long lines at the camp water tap.*

▼ *In Afghanistan, most people have no gas or electricity and depend on firewood for heating and cooking. As the area around the city becomes deforested, boys bike into the countryside to collect whatever they can find, either for their family to use or to sell.*

▲ *These children in Sierra Leone crack open palm kernels, which can be processed for their rich oil. The children are contributing to the family income by doing this repetitive job, leaving their parents free to farm their land. After fighting stopped, fields were overgrown and needed a lot of work to return them to productive use.*

▲ *Maryam and her granddaughter collect small sticks to use as kindling from their wheat field in the Herat province of Afghanistan.*

AFGHANISTAN

The poverty that accompanies war means children often become breadwinners for their families. This is especially the case in Afghanistan. The large number of widows means that children, particularly boys, have the responsibility of earning some cash—perhaps by carrying goods in the market or minding animals. Girls, like Majan, often weave, as this painstaking work, which needs small nimble fingers, can be done in the home.

> When I was sixteen, I got married. I'd already lost my father and brothers during the war. After one year of marriage, my husband was killed in fighting, so I came back to my mother's house. To earn some money to help my mother, I went to another house to weave, but now I'm much happier because I have a loom at home and I can weave at home and then sell the carpets. I make sixteen-foot- (five-meter-) long ones which sell for sixty dollars.

In Kabul, Afghanistan's capital, I've seen little gangs of children carrying sacks as big as themselves. Sometimes they collect wastepaper and plastic to sell to recyclers. Other times it's twigs in the park to use as kindling. Children also go to bread shops to collect stale naan. This traditional bread goes hard very quickly. What isn't sold within a few hours is often given to the poor. Bread with weak tea is the basic meal for thousands of people in poverty, especially for those who have fled to the cities for safety from the fighting and have no land on which to grow food.

▶ *In desperate times, people take desperate measures. In a marketplace in Kurdistan, I saw this tiny girl, an Iraqi refugee from the south, selling chewing gum, rather unwillingly. Her mother had sent her out, thinking people would feel sorry for her and buy something.*

WORKING CHILDREN

Almost 25 percent of Afghan children age 7–14 work.

Source: UNICEF 2009 Facts on child protection in Afghanistan.

▼ *Majan, age nineteen, is a skilled carpet weaver.*

▲ When the Taliban came to power in 1996, they banned kite flying, among other things. Now, ten-year-old Jamil is able to help in his father's workshop in Kabul. On Fridays (Afghanistan's day of rest), boys have kite-flying competitions.

THE PHOTOGRAPHER'S PERSPECTIVE

Watching children weaving, I am overwhelmed that, even though they have never been to school and can't read or write, they can interpret a pattern on paper into a carpet. On the street, child vendors can calculate change without ever having taken a math class.

A young boy minding sheep or goats is responsible for the animals in his care. He has to cope with being by himself all day and make sure no animal is lost, injured, or stolen, as he could never afford to replace it.

While I'm impressed by the skills working children have, I'm depressed by their lost childhood. They have almost no time for play. Hasmatullah, a weaver, told me about his life.

▲ *Hasmatullah, age fourteen. There are ten in his family: two parents, a grandmother, three brothers and three sisters.*

I am the only one earning money in my family. My father was disabled in the war. A land mine exploded and he lost his hand. We were refugees in Iran, and six years ago we returned to Kabul. When we could no longer pay the rent, we moved out of the city. Afghan children were not allowed to go to school in Iran, so I do not know how to read or write. I have been training to weave for six months and earning an income for my family. I earn three dollars a day, and when I finish the training, I hope I will find work as a trainee carpet weaver in Kabul. ❞

◀ *Ibrahim sells sweet potatoes by the roadside in Sierra Leone.*

32

▲ *In the center of Kabul, Afghanistan, it's hard to find anywhere for animals to graze other than among the trash piled by the road. Looking after animals here means coping with traffic, too.*

CASE STUDY: PHOTOVOICE PROJECT, PAKISTAN, 2010

In Pakistan, many families have fled the danger of the northern states—brought by the war in Afghanistan—for big cities farther south. In areas such as Rawalpindi, thousands of children end up working in order for their families to survive. I spent a couple of weeks on a PhotoVoice project teaching photography to working children, who produced an exhibition about their lives.

▲ Girls Scavenging, *by Sitara, who wrote, "These children are collecting rubbish, but they should be going to school."*

▲ Boy in a Workshop, *by Hikmat, who wrote, "This is Ibrahim, he's twelve. He used to come and study at this center but then his parents insisted he went out to work."*

SCHOOL AND PLAY

For some children, the violence that war brings completely disrupts their education, destroying or closing schools. For those who make it into a camp, classes may be organized by international agencies such as the United Nations Children's Fund (UNICEF), Save the Children, or Islamic Relief. These classes help provide some structure for children traumatized by the loss of their home and familiar surroundings. For some children this is their first experience of school.

▲ *In 2007, when I visited schools in camps for IDPs in Darfur, no one moaned about having gym class in the boiling hot desert.*

Usually, the teachers are volunteers from the camp itself and understand the problems of concentration and distress that the pupils may face. The classes are often overcrowded, but the students appreciate having something to do.

KURDISTAN, 2008

In Kurdistan, the Iraqi children I met at a muddy camp were enrolled in local schools. This had many benefits: they met local children, they had trained teachers, and they had a school with reasonable facilities.

But there were also negative points. Children struggled with the language because everything was in Kurdish rather than Arabic, the language of southern Iraq. They were also embarrassed about where they lived. They were surrounded by mud, making it difficult for them to keep their uniforms clean.

◄ *This little girl had put plastic bags over her shoes so that they wouldn't be too muddy by the time she reached school.*

▲ *Grace was abducted from her school and forced to walk to Sudan. The experience of having to be the "wife" of a boy soldier has traumatized her, and made it hard for her to return to her village. Everyone knows what happened to her, but she has nowhere else to go.*

UGANDA, 2007

In northern Uganda, the LRA specifically abducted large numbers of boarding-school students. Nearly all high schools have boarders (children who stay at school overnight) because the distances between the school and their homes are too great. The abducted children became LRA fighters, "wives," cooks, and manual laborers.

GAZA, 2009

I went to Gaza just after the Israeli Operation Cast Lead. The three weeks of war resulted in more than one thousand Palestinian and thirteen Israeli deaths (four from "friendly fire"). A number of schools were destroyed by the bombing, but children returned to classes as soon as there was a cease-fire. Many had to study in temporary classrooms while theirs were being repaired.

▼ *Many children find it hard to speak about their experiences, but find drawing a helpful way to express bottled-up emotions.*

▲ *Children gingerly make their way to school through a street lined with badly damaged buildings.*

35

SWAT VALLEY, PAKISTAN, 2005

I traveled to remote villages in the Swat Valley of Pakistan, near the Afghan border, where an organization named Khwendo Kor was coordinating classes in homes and courtyards. In one school that I visited, the young teacher, whose only qualification was that she had completed primary school, had nothing more than a blackboard and a few books, but the students couldn't have been more enthusiastic. They sat in the hot sun concentrating on gaining knowledge. Girls realize that education is the only way for them to avoid a lifetime of isolation in their homes, where the only people they would meet would be their husband, children, and female relatives.

These lessons were allowed only after long meetings with the community elders, but everyone was fearful and unsure of the future safety of their classes. One teacher had already been shot and left for dead. When a newspaper published the story and printed her name, some of her family disowned her, believing she had brought shame on them.

▼ *Supporters of Malala demonstrate outside the British Prime Minister's home in London, England, in October 2012.*

▲▶ *A teacher and pupil at a Khwendo Kor class.*

In October 2012, fifteen-year-old Pakistani schoolgirl Malala Yousafzai was shot in the head and chest by the Taliban. She had campaigned for the right for girls to have education. People all over the world were outraged and realized that, in many places, education is a right that has to be fought for. Malala became a worldwide icon and made people aware of the plight of girls in her country and elsewhere. Malala was not the first, or only, schoolgirl to be attacked. Girls in Pakistan have had acid thrown at them at various times over the last twenty years, teachers have been killed, and ninety-six schools were damaged or destroyed in 2012. In 2011 the figure was even higher, at one hundred and fifty-two.

Of the 235 pupils at this school, 136 are girls.

▲ *Children head inside to begin their lessons at a primary school in Shomali Plain, 2006.*

AFGHANISTAN, 2006

Girls living in rural areas never had much access to education, but under the Taliban (1996–2001) all girls were forbidden to attend school. In spite of this, hundreds of pupils carried on studying in small groups at private homes. After the Taliban was ousted by North Atlantic Treaty Organization (NATO) forces, girls' education was considered a priority and new schools were built.

Unfortunately, not everyone agreed with such equality. Some schools were burned down, teachers were intimidated, and there were even instances where school lunches and water were poisoned in girls' schools. Despite a climate of fear, girls' education is now flourishing and, along with studying, many are playing sports, including soccer, basketball, and boxing.

▶ *Girls enjoy skipping rope at their new school.*

When a country goes to war, schools soon close. Children may have a lot of time to play, but nothing to play with, or they may be stuck at home because it's too dangerous to go out. However, some wars do lead to new opportunities for children. NGOs might set up activities, including pottery and art classes, for displaced children and refugees.

When families flee into exile, they are unlikely to include toys among the few possessions they take. Children often make their own toys from scrap materials they find lying around.

▼ *These Sierra Leonean boys scratch out their own game board on the ground.*

▲ *Boys in the CAR make their own soccer balls from scrap plastic tied tightly with crisscrossed string.*

▼ *All over Africa, children enjoy hoop rolling, using whatever they can find for the hoop. This boy was playing in a refugee camp in Goma, DRC, in 2008.*

◄ This young girl was living on a landfill site in Kurdistan. She found this doll in the trash there.

Qamar, a Syrian refugee living in the Za'atri camp in Jordan, lamented how her life changed.

" Before the war started we spent our time playing outside the house, but after it started we had to stay in all the time. We missed a lot of school — sometimes we only went once a week. Sometimes, we'd only be there an hour before we'd have to leave. A few times on our way home from school, there was shooting and we'd have to hide in a house. "

Children in different parts of the world have different expectations. Teenage refugees from Syria, accustomed to computers and electronic games, found it difficult when the only electronic devices their family had were solar lamps. But children are incredibly resourceful and are often able to make a game out of virtually nothing at all. In Jordan, I saw a little Syrian girl playing with a water bottle. She had dressed it in a red T-shirt and it was now her doll.

Hanifa attempts an "ollie" on her skateboard outside her home.

▲ *These Lebanese children have been sent Hula-Hoops and jump ropes by Save the Children.*

Charities that work with children have realized the importance of organizing safe play areas within refugee camps, both to keep children busy and to stop them from thinking too much about what they have lost. This may be as simple as helping teenagers organize games for younger children or it may be building a whole playground. It all comes down to funding. If a charity can raise enough money, it may supply Hula-Hoops, swings, and art supplies.

AFGHANISTAN, 2011

There is now a thriving skateboard community in Kabul, thanks to the NGO Skateistan. Skateistan opened in 2009 and offers children free skateboarding lessons. It also provides opportunities for children to take part in classroom activities and has around 350 students, just under half of which are girls. I met Hanifa (left), the proud owner of a skateboard, who was eager to show me her skills. Living on a mountainside means that she has very little space to practice. She has a long walk to the park where she sells snacks, so she doesn't have much spare time.

▲ *Girls in Chad enthusiastically played with a volleyball, a donation from an aid organization.*

THE PHOTOGRAPHER'S FINAL THOUGHTS

"
It is a privilege to be a photographer.
It can be exciting to be present when history is made, but it is also soul-destroying to earn a living from photographing misery and devastation. It's heartening when peace agreements are signed, warring factions forget their grievances, and life can get back to relative normality. "

As a photographer I have to be careful with the photos I take. Pictures can be seen around the world once they are on the Internet, with no way to control who sees them. In some cultures, it is considered inappropriate for girls to be photographed. Even though a girl might be happy to have pictures taken, her family might not. In a volatile conflict, photos might be incriminating and used against the subject.

As photography has become cheaper and faster with the use of digital cameras and phones, people directly involved in a war have increasingly been able to photograph and film it themselves. There is always the problem of verification, distinguishing between news and propaganda, because photos—like words—are always subjective.

If you had to choose one single photo to sum up *Children Growing Up with War,* which of these would you choose?

CASE STUDY: STUDENTS' PHOTOGRAPHY PROJECT

Photography can be a powerful tool for change. This was vividly brought home to me when I facilitated a photography workshop for young people in Afghanistan, who produced an exhibition on the rights of the child.

▲ The Right to Health, *by Mansoor*

"This is Mursal playing in a puddle. She is poor. She has no elder brother, but elder sisters."

▲ The Right to Education, *by Sesai*

▲ The Right to be Heard, *by Maryam*

"This photo shows that people are now free after a lot of war. Now we can learn and play and have fun."

▲ *One of my students photographs a shoe-shine boy.*

43

MAP OF CONFLICTS

This map shows the countries referred to in this book. With the exception of the U.K. and Vietnam, all are currently in conflict.

GAZA
pages 13, 14, 35

U.K.
page 25

TUNISIA
pages 10, 14, 46

LIBYA
pages 10, 14, 46

CHAD
pages 3, 12, 41, 46

SIERRA LEONE
pages 18, 22, 29, 32, 38, 47

DARFUR
pages 12, 34, 46

THE DRC
pages 6, 7, 18, 21, 23, 26, 38, 46, 47

LEBANON
pages 8, 9, 25, 46, 47

SYRIA
pages 11, 20, 26, 39, 47

AFGHANISTAN
pages 4, 15, 16, 17, 23, 24, 27, 28, 29, 30, 31, 32, 33, 37, 40, 41, 43, 46

JORDAN
pages 11, 20, 26, 39, 47

PAKISTAN
pages 33, 36, 46

IRAQ
pages 3, 13, 14, 24, 30, 34, 46, 47

VIETNAM
page 5

SUDAN
pages 3, 12, 35, 46, 47

UGANDA
pages 3, 18, 19, 35, 46, 47

RWANDA
pages 21, 23, 46, 47

THE MAIN CONFLICTS

AFGHANISTAN

Afghanistan has been in conflict since the Soviet Union invaded it in 1979 to support its pro-communist regime. After the Soviets withdrew in 1989, civil war broke out between competing groups. In 1996, the Islamic fundamentalist movement know as the Taliban took power, imposing strict Islamic law. This was especially harsh on women, who were not allowed to work, leave home, or go to school. Following the 9/11 terrorist attacks on the United States, the U.S. invaded Afghanistan and overthrew the Taliban. The country has, however, remained in conflict, and civilians fled the violence. Today, more than 2.7 million Afghans live in exile, mainly in Pakistan and Iran. Afghanistan's living standards are among the lowest in the world. In many areas, there is a shortage of housing, clean water, electricity, medical care, and jobs.

DARFUR

For decades, life in Darfur, in western Sudan, has been precarious. Drought and food shortages have led to local conflicts over land and water. Civil war erupted in 2003 when rebels attacked government targets, accusing the government in Khartoum of neglecting black Africans in favor of Arabs. In response, the government-backed Arab Janjaweed militia attacked and razed Darfur's black African villages, killing many inhabitants. Hundreds of thousands fled to Chad, Uganda, Kenya, and Ethiopia. The conflict continues. More than 1.4 million people (one fifth of the population) remain homeless, living in refugee camps. Hundreds of thousands of children have been born in camps and have known no other life.

DEMOCRATIC REPUBLIC OF THE CONGO (DRC)

In 1998, two armed rebel groups in the DRC, a huge central-African country, attacked the Congolese army and started a deadly conflict for political power and control of the country's rich mineral resources. Other African countries were drawn in. Angola, Namibia, and Zimbabwe supported the army and Rwandan, Ugandan, and Burundi troops supported the rebels. During the war, which lasted until 2003, an estimated 5.4 million people died—90 percent of them due to disease and famine. Almost half of the deaths were of children under the age of fifteen. Two million people were internally displaced, and hundreds of thousands who fled the country sought refuge in camps near the border. Today, there is renewed violence as armed rebel groups still clash. Civilians are still at risk from attack and continue to flee the country.

IRAQ

U.S., U.K., Australian and Polish troops invaded Iraq in 2003 to depose Saddam Hussein, the Iraqi ruler, and prevent his use of suspected nuclear weapons (weapons of mass destruction), which the U.S. and its allies claimed posed a threat to Western security. The toppling of Saddam's government led to years of internal fighting as conflicting groups competed for power. More than 4.5 million children lost one or both parents in the war. Seventy percent of schools were damaged or destroyed. Thousands of teachers and doctors fled overseas. Economic collapse led to increased poverty and malnutrition and the development of more slums. Toxic heavy metals in modern weaponry are causing serious health problems and have led to birth defects. U.S. troops left in 2011, but unrest, sectarian tension, and violence continue.

LEBANON

In 2006, a thirty-four-day conflict occurred between Hezbollah (a Shia Islamic militant group in Lebanon) and Israel. Hezbollah fighters captured two Israeli soldiers and killed several more in a cross-border raid. Outraged, Israel responded with bombs and missile strikes on towns, ports, power plants, and the airport, leaving people without food, water, or electricity. Tens of thousands of homes were destroyed or damaged. Hezbollah launched rockets into northern Israel and waged guerrilla warfare with Israeli forces. More than a million Lebanese and up to half a million Israelis fled their homes. After the ceasefire, some parts of southern Lebanon were uninhabitable because of unexploded Israeli cluster bombs.

LIBYA

Colonel Muammar Gaddafi ruled oil-rich Libya for more than forty years. In 2011, anti-government Libyans staged demonstrations, demanding change. Peaceful protest rapidly escalated into armed rebellion as the government and rebel forces fought for control of major towns. Thousands of people fled to temporary shelter in Tunisia to escape the violence. After some months, the rebels stormed Libya's capital city Tripoli and, several weeks later, Gaddafi was captured and killed in his hometown. A transitional government took charge, until elections for a General National Congress were held in 2012. This marked the country's first free national election in six decades. There is still sporadic violence, and thousands of people have not been able to return home.

RWANDA

There had long been animosity between the majority Hutus and minority Tutsis of Rwanda. In 1994, Hutus blamed Tutsis for the death of the Hutu president, whose plane was shot down. Over the next one hundred days, unofficial Hutu militia, soldiers, policemen, and ordinary civilians slaughtered hundreds of thousands of Tutsis with machetes, clubs, and knives. The genocide ended when the Rwandan Patriotic Front (RPF), a military force of exiled Tutsis, took over the country. Fearing retribution, two million Hutus fled to the DRC. Thousands died of diseases that spread quickly in overcrowded camps.

SIERRA LEONE

Civil war raged between 1991 and 2002 in this diamond-rich country. Rebels tried to overthrow successive governments, accusing them of corruption and mismanagement of the country's vast mineral resources. In a campaign of terror, the rebels murdered, looted, raped, and mutilated innocent civilians. They abducted thousands of children for use as soldiers, laborers, or "wives." The UN intervened in 1999, persuading both sides to sign a peace agreement. Peacekeeping forces disarmed the rebels. In 2007, three rebel leaders were sentenced to long jail terms for the civil-war atrocities.

SYRIA

In 2011, protests against President Bashar al-Assad, whose family has ruled Syria for more than forty years, were met with a lethal crackdown by government troops. The protests rapidly escalated into civil war across the country. More than 80,000 civilians have been killed. Almost 4 million Syrians have fled their homes, either to safer places in Syria, or across the border to Jordan, Turkey, or Lebanon. Syria has been home to a large number of urban refugees from Iraq and elsewhere. These people have also had to flee, often back to unsafe futures in their own countries.

UGANDA

Initially founded as a militia claiming to defend the Acholi people in northern Uganda, the Lord's Resistance Army (LRA) has become a personality cult around its present leader, Joseph Kony. Known for its brutality, the LRA carried out vicious attacks in remote regions, murdering most of the adult population, mutilating the rest, and abducting children. Boys became fighters. Girls became sex slaves. Eventually forced out of the country by the Ugandan army, the LRA has moved into the Democratic Republic of the Congo, the Central African Republic, and southern Sudan, where it continues its savage raids.

WEBSITES

www.actionaid.org
Find out about ActionAid's projects, helping poor and marginalized people to eradicate poverty and overcome injustice and inequity in more than forty-five countries.

www.baobabsurvivors.org
Read about how Baobab helps children and young people who have fled from political violence, torture, and family loss in more than twenty war-torn countries.

www.care-international.org
Learn how CARE International provides civilians in war zones with places to go for food, shelter, and support and helps the world's poorest people find routes out of poverty.

www.islamic-relief.com
Find out about the projects run across the world by Islamic Relief as they tackle the suffering of the world's poorest people.

www.khwendokor.org.pk
Discover the projects run by Khwendo Kor, which helps improve the health, education, and skills of women and children in two poor, remote areas of Pakistan.

www.merlin.org.uk
Learn about how Merlin (now part of Save the Children) sends doctors and nurses to global emergencies to save lives and care for the injured, as well as how it helps to improve the health of people who have suffered from war or famine.

www.msf.org
Find out what immediate and longer-term humanitarian medical aid Médecins Sans Frontières provides for victims of conflict and natural disasters.

www.photovoice.org
See how PhotoVoice works with NGOs around the world to give disadvantaged people the chance to represent themselves and create tools for positive social change.

www.savethechildren.net
Find out how Save the Children ensures that children affected by war get food, clean water, and medical aid, as well as giving them safe places to learn and play.

www.skateistan.org
Be inspired by Skateistan, which uses skateboarding to engage hard-to-reach Afghan youth and provides them with education, skills, and cross-cultural interaction.

www.unhcr.org
Research how the United Nations Refugee Agency coordinates action to safeguard the rights and well-being of refugees and resolve refugee problems worldwide.

GLOSSARY

baad a way of settling disputes between Afghan families by giving away a girl to the family of the victim of a crime

bride price money, goods, or property that a husband's family gives to his wife's family when they marry

cholera an acute bacterial infection caused by drinking contaminated water, which can be fatal

civil war a war between people within the same country

defoliant a chemical that makes plant leaves fall off

fixer a local person with good contacts

friendly fire when a military force is fired upon from one's own side

fundamentalist one who supports a religious movement that believes in interpreting its sacred text as truth

genocide the systematic, deliberate killing of a large number of a particular racial or cultural group

human rights the basic freedoms to which all humans are entitled, including life, liberty, thought, expression, and equality

immunization protective vaccination against diseases such as polio, measles, mumps, rubella, and diphtheria

internally displaced person (IDP) someone forced to flee their home, but who remains within their own country

land mine an explosive charge, hidden just under the ground, designed to blast enemy targets as they pass over it

malaria a fever, often fatal for children, caused by a parasite and spread by the bite of an infected mosquito

national service short-term compulsory participation in the armed services during peacetime

rebel someone who resists an established government, often with armed force

reconciliation the re-establishment of friendly relations between opposing groups after a conflict

refugees people forced to move to another country when they no longer feel safe in their own, because of war, religious persecution, or natural disaster

Shia a branch of Islam followed by 20 percent of the world's Muslims

Sunni the mainstream branch of Islam, followed by 80 percent of the world's Muslims

Taliban an extreme Islamic group that seized power in Afghanistan and imposed a strict Muslim regime

INDEX